EMPOWER ... ENCOURAGE ... EMBRACE
YOUR

Strong Girl Spirit

21 DAYS OF PLANTING & GROWING SEEDS OF STRENGTH

THIS JOURNAL BELONGS TO

_ _ _ _ _ _ _ _ _ _ _ _ _ _ _ _

First Edition

Strong Girl Enterprises

www.stronggirlspirit.com

ISBN: 978-1-0932728-3-3

Design by Margaret Cogswell
margaretcogswell.com

THIS BOOK IS DEDICATED TO ALL THE "STRONG GIRLS" IN MY LIFE.

The ladies that have inspired me and continue to inspire me every day with amazing support, strength, humor, beauty, and unconditional love.
YOU ALL HOLD THE TRUE SPIRIT OF A STRONG GIRL!

Monica Peters, Daughter

Rylee Peters, Granddaughter

Desi Peters, Granddaughter

Aunt Beba Smereck, Aunt

Mary Jones, like a daughter

Watching over us in Heaven:

My Beautiful Mom (Tiny)
& Grandma Tina

And last but certainly not least...
Grandma Ruby (the original Strong Girl)

and to the following amazing men and other people in my life...

that have made a difference with their
support, patience, love and humor.

Dean Peters, Son

Bill Paulson, Brother

Rick Paulson, Brother

Dad Paulson, Dad

Kelly Peters (Awesome Dad to our children)

Tom Bowyer (Dear Friend & Confidant)

Gary Waschow (Mentor & Amazing Friend)
& last but not least...

Eric Nathan (Soul-mate, husband, and love, you bought my "rocking chairs")

And all the many "Dream" teams I have had the pleasure to partner and work with over my many years.

(You know who you are)

a special note to the amazing parents of all the strong girls out there.

I'm sure you already know this,
but it is worth repeating, as repetition is our friend.

Children learn by example, by what we do, what we say, and who we are.

Our children are **always listening, always watching and always learning.**

You (Mom, Dad, Aunt, Uncle, Grandma, and Grandpa) are always on stage
and **you take center stage in your child's world.**

Pay attention to your attitude and body language towards others,
towards yourself & towards the world around you.

Answer your children's questions honestly. There is a "Strong Girl" in all girls.
Take an active role in planting and growing the seeds of strength,
acceptance, and respect in your Strong Girl.

Your show of strength about yourself is her model.

Every positive word you plant in your child needs
watering and **you hold the water bucket.**

Help to reinforce these powerful words of strength, daily, in your Strong Girl.

Dear Strong Girl,

What you focus on grows!

Have you ever planted a seed in the ground? Even if you haven't, the only way the seed grows into a flower, or a vegetable or fruit, is to water it daily and to care for it.

We are the same, we are growing and learning every day, if we don't feed ourselves with daily positive thoughts, we won't grow and be the best we can be.

It takes practice, in the same way you learned to ride a bike, learned to walk, learned to play a sport or instrument, or even tie your shoes, it's the small, daily positive steps over and over again that build your daily habit of positive strength.

Positive words give life and the positive seeds you plant within yourself will begin to shape the way you see yourself and the world, in a good way.

Each day as you read your daily seeds of strength, you will become stronger and stronger. Each day you will be reminding yourself just how amazing you are.

But be careful, because just like a flower, sometimes weeds will get in the way. Sometimes our weeds are negative friends, family, bullies, and maybe even sometimes ourselves.

So, when the weeds of life around you start popping up, you will need to feed yourself with more positive seeds of strength.

There are two things we can control:
1. The way we feel, and
2. The way we think.

You can't control how someone else acts or behaves, just like you can't control if it rains or if it's sunny outside. You can only control how you feel about it and how you react to the situation at hand.

Strong Girls...

Stand up for themselves

Take charge of how you feel

Reality check: Ask, "Does it really matter?"

Own it; own how you feel about it

Notice how you are feeling in the moment, acknowledge the feeling, and then choose to move on

Get your cape of confidence on...

You are the ONLY superhero you need. Put on your cape of confidence, you have the power to be YOU, be Confident, be strong!

There is beauty in strength of mind and thoughts, you've got this Strong Girl!

xoxo,

Terrie Nathan

\- - - - - - - - -

HOW TO GET THE MOST OUT OF THIS DAILY JOURNEY

Like I mentioned, building positive habits takes time, so over the next 21 days we will plant **daily** positive seeds in your life. Try reading your seeds of strength, once in the morning and again before you go to bed.

Along the way you will also be able to **journal** and log **"cape of confidence thoughts"** to further add to your growth, motivation, and strength.

Daily Strong Girl motivation will put a smile on your face and touch the hearts of others in your life.

How you feel and act is contagious and as you plant your seeds of daily strength you will grow, gain more confidence, be grateful, and get stronger every day.

Your **light of strength** will shine bright!

Empower ... Encourage ... Embrace your words.

_ _ _ _ _ _ _ _ _

Have you planted your "Strong Girl Seeds of Strength" today?

When you see that means repeat out loud.

The more you repeat the "I Am's" the stronger you get.
Answer the questions, journal your thoughts, write down your feelings.

Use the sticky notes to post in your room, or put on your mirror or in your book. The more you see the words of strength, the more you grow and build your muscle of positive thinking.

Finally, pass on the positive! Use the same stickers to plant seeds of strength into someone else. Now go out and be the best version of you, Strong Girl.

use your check in chart!

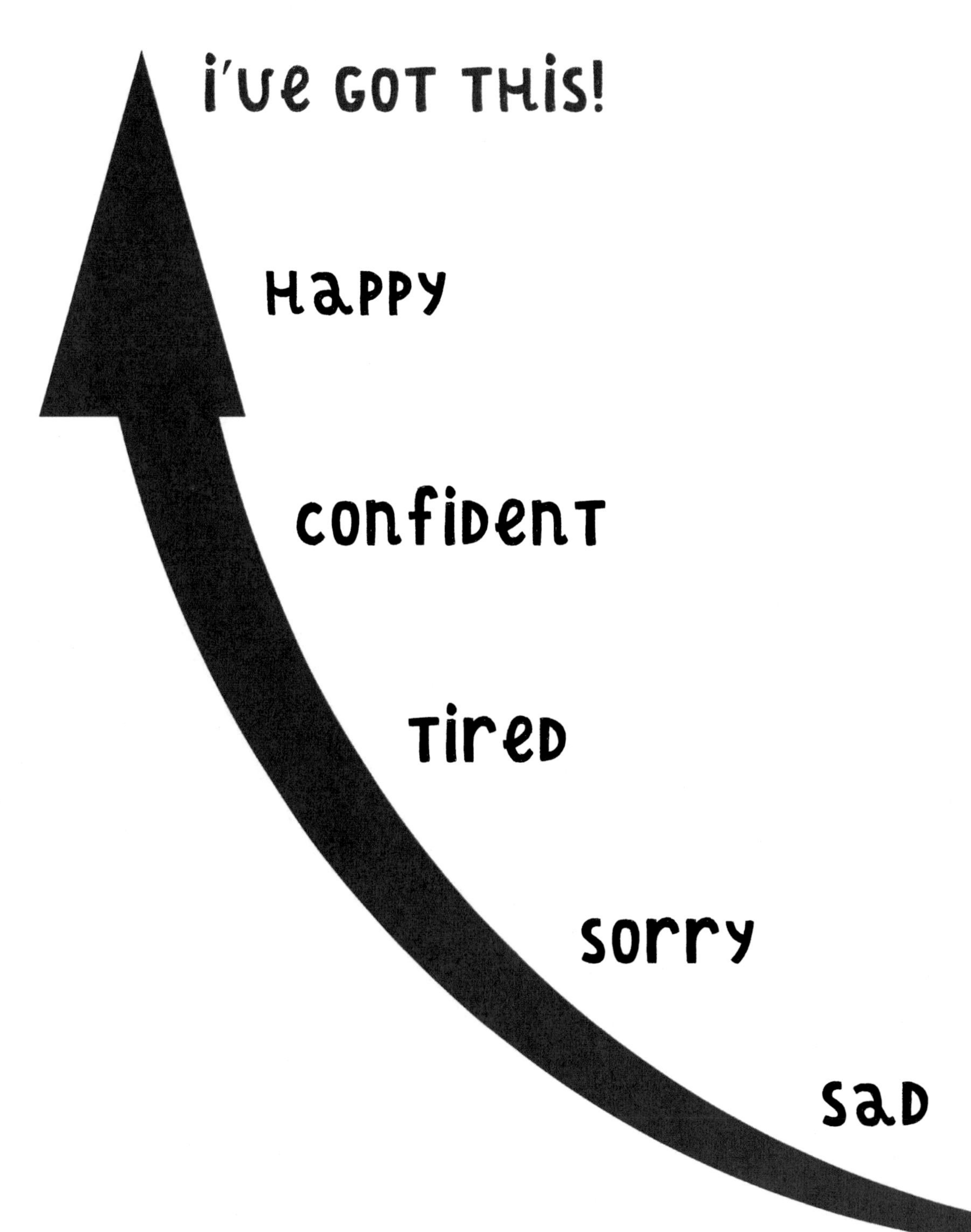

Where are you emotionally? What can you do to climb up the curve of strength?

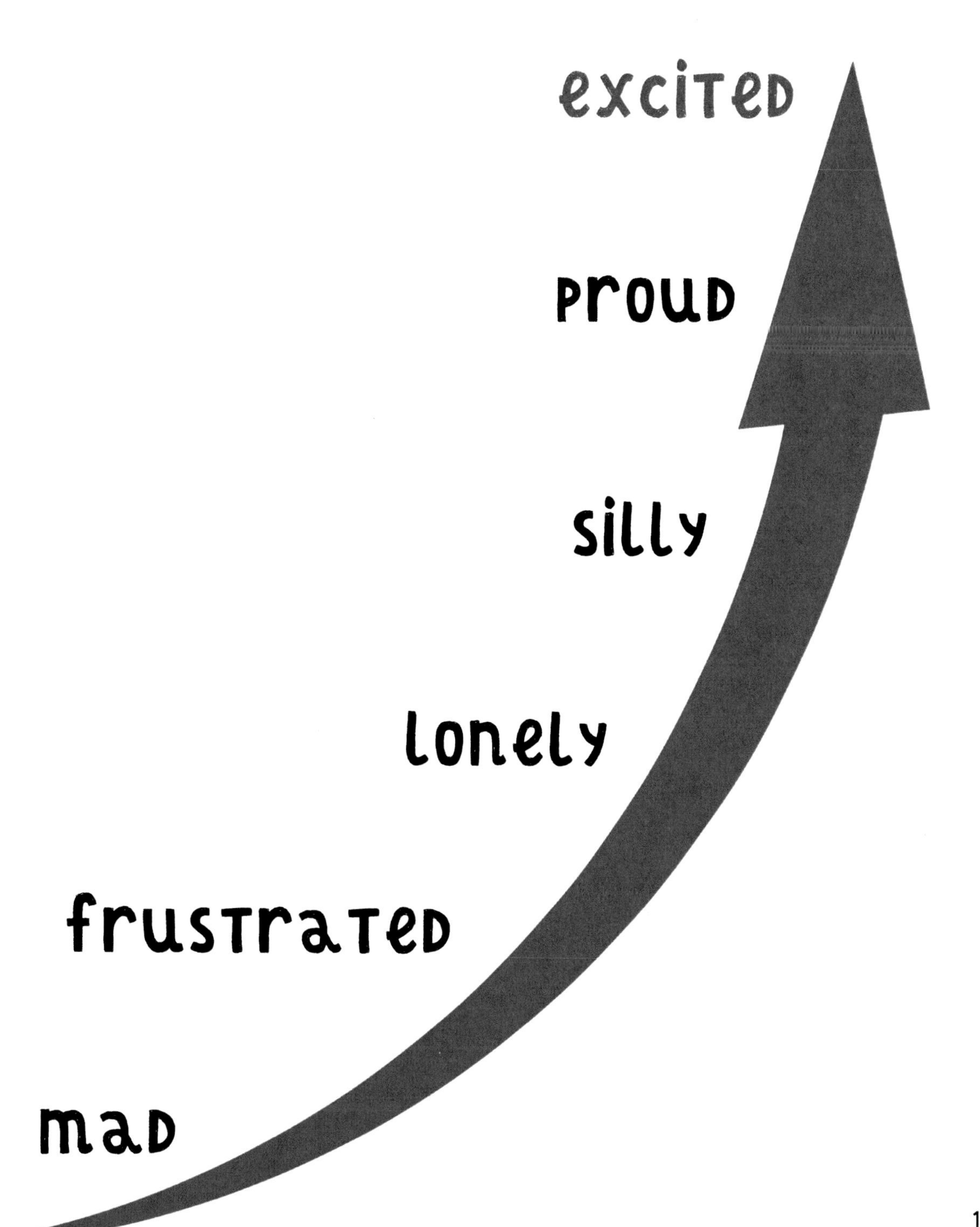

are you ready to
start your journey,
strong girl?

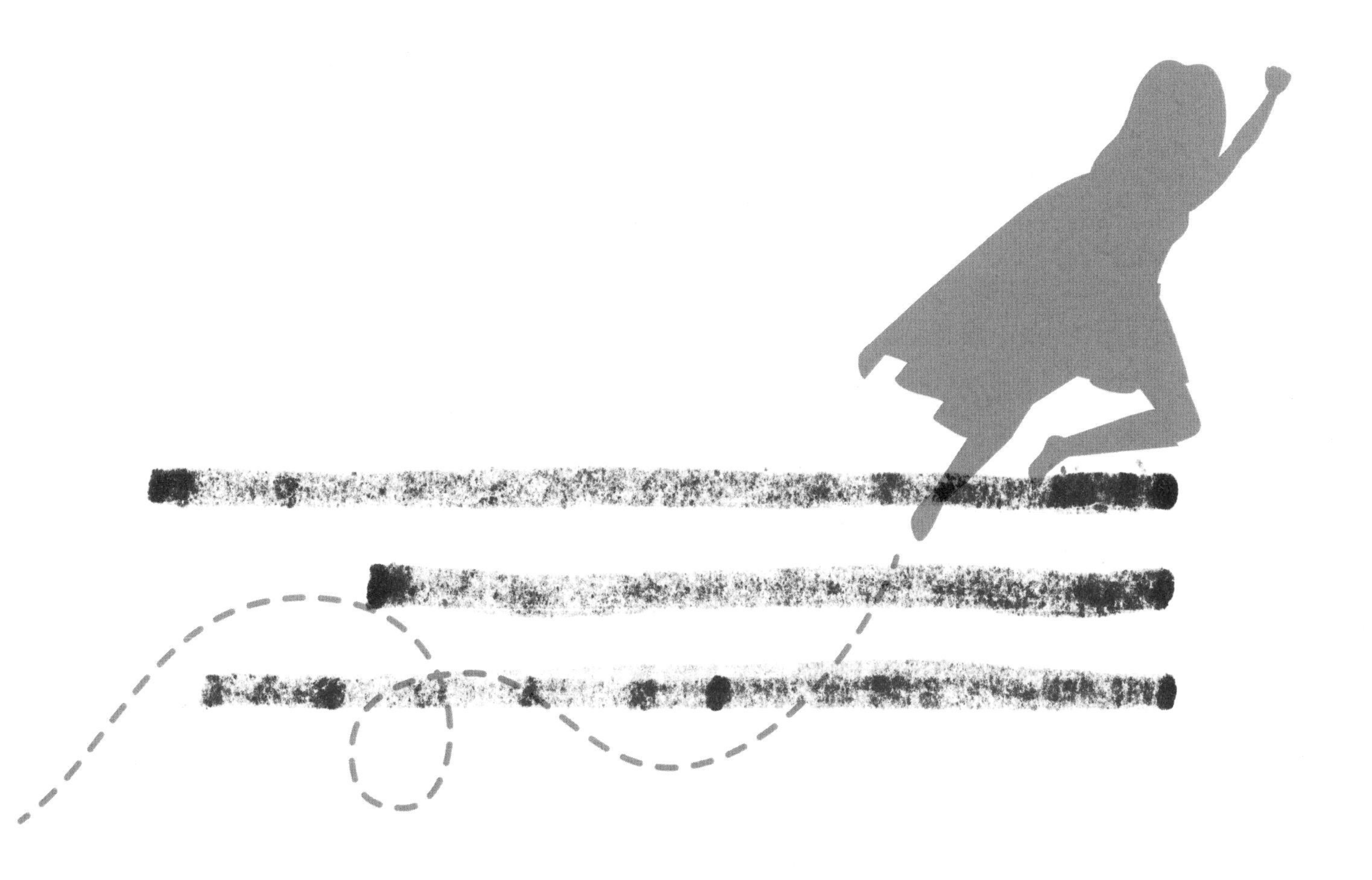

GOOD MORNING, STRONG GIRL.

WELCOME TO

Day one

I am amazing.

I am amazing.

I am amazing.

THE MOST IMPORTANT THING A GIRL WEARS IS HER CONFIDENCE.

We are what we say we are ... **you are** amazing.

Dear Strong Girl, it is ok to be comfortable with who you are.
It's about being you and loving the AMAZING YOU that YOU are!

Now write two things that you think make you amazing. Since this is your first exercise, it might be tough to think of two, but think big! I know you are amazing, you just need to write it down! Write down more if you want, but write at least two.

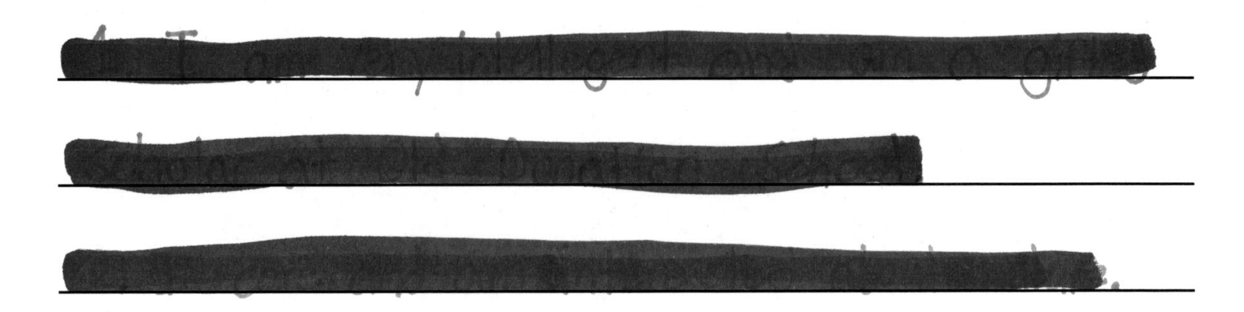

Now the next step: while at school or church, while playing with friends, your brother, your sister, your mom, your dad, or the family pet, tell them why you think they are amazing. Because you know what Strong Girl? They are amazing, just like you.

Lessons LEARNED

I am amazing.

I can remember a time when I had to dress up for a special event at school. I didn't have much to pick from at the time, but I did have this one dress my grandma made for me.

When I showed up for the event, some girls starting laughing and asking me how I got that "dumb dress." All of the sudden I was so embarrassed to be wearing it. Just at that moment a teacher came by and whispered in my ear, "**You are amazing**, now just keep on saying it to yourself!" She said, "You can just erase those mean words with a your pretend 'pink eraser.'" So I did, I erased them and then I kept running those three words, "you are amazing," through my mind.

It worked and I no longer felt stupid or ugly because I was wearing a dress others didn't like. I was so proud and happy that this dress I was wearing was a one of a kind dress. And in that moment I was Strong Girl. Those words have stuck with me.

I AM amazing and so are you!

If you don't like the words that are spoken to you, then change the words you speak to yourself. Choose words of positivity. Pull out your mental 'pink eraser' and erase the words that are not positive!

Trust me, it works.

Lessons LEARNED

I am strong.

We all want to fit in and to be like the cool kids. I know that's what I always wanted, was to just fit in, but it seemed I never could. But what does that mean, really?

Well, you know what? I am so glad that I was different, that I am different, and that I am cool in my own way. Being strong doesn't just mean to have strong muscles. Being strong means being strong in your thoughts. It means to be proud of who you are, love your flaws, love your quirks, love how your nose wrinkles when you smile. Be strong in self.

Because I didn't fit in as a young girl, I struggled to see my strength. I was very lucky as a young girl to have a grandma that spoke positive words of favor into my life. When I would visit her she would always tell me how beautiful, kind, and loving I was. She always called me her Strong Girl and would ask me who I was, and I would respond, "I AM Strong Girl."

These positive words have stuck with me and continue to move me through days, even when I am struggling with something.

Try it ... **I AM Strong Girl ... I AM Strong Girl.**

GOOD MORNING, STRONG GIRL.

WELCOME TO

Day TWO

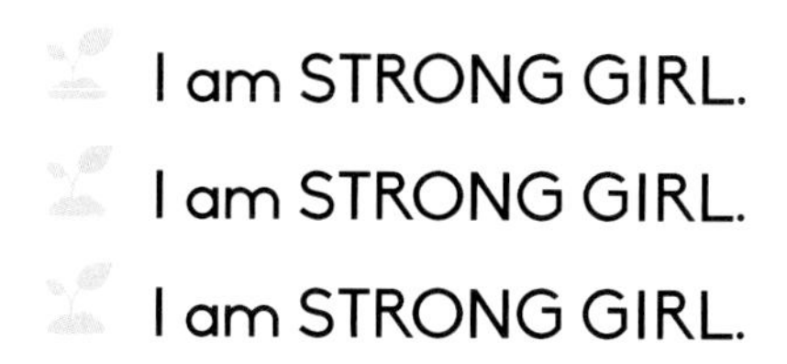

I am STRONG GIRL.

I am STRONG GIRL.

I am STRONG GIRL.

It's easy to let things overwhelm you, however in tough times you have to stay strong. You must look for the positive. Keep the right attitude and you will quickly see just how strong you can be in any situation. You are strong in mind, body and your spirit.

List 2-3 things that make you **amazing and strong**.

GOOD MORNING, STRONG GIRL.

WELCOME TO

Day Three

- I am patient.
- I am patient.
- I am patient.

Act, don't react. Sometimes things just happen.
It's important to have patience and respond with the right attitude.

Sometimes you will be put into situations to test your patience.

Write down an example of where you have had to be patient and maybe write down a time when you weren't patient. What did you learn from it?

Pass the test. Be Patient.

GOOD MORNING, STRONG GIRL.

WELCOME TO

Day four

- I am energetic.
- I am energetic.
- I am energetic.

Even if I am tired, I am Strong Girl and I get up and get my energy going. I eat right, I get plenty of rest, and get plenty of activity.

What are some things or activities that you do to keep your energy up? What time do you go to bed?

Getting rest is important if you want to be a Strong Girl.

Lessons LEARNED

I am beautiful. I am beautiful. I am beautiful.

When you see celebrities or pictures of models all with the same body type, it's easy to think that is what normal looks like. But what is normal? Whose definition of normal are you using? How about using your own definition of normal, or how about real?

The world is filled with people of all sizes and all shapes and everyone in their own way is beautiful. Celebrate your kind, silly, quirky, crazy, fun, unique you. This is who you are, this is how you were made, so celebrate your real, unique inner beauty. Beauty is really on the inside looking out! And Strong Girls embrace who they are.

Focus on being healthy. Wear clothes that make you feel good about yourself. Get plenty of rest and exercise, as this is what drives your healthy attitude. I have learned over the years that when I focus on how I feel, instead of what a scale or a number might say, I all of the sudden feel amazing.

I also surround myself with positive people who make me feel good, because they feel good. Most importantly, push this message of the new beauty to other girls. When you feel good, pay that feeling forward to your friends and family, I can't think of any reason not to!

GOOD MORNING, STRONG GIRL.

WELCOME TO

Day five

I am beautiful.

I am beautiful.

I am beautiful.

"Why fit in when you were born to stand out?" -Dr. Suess

You have a beautiful smile, you have a beautiful personality, you have beautiful eyes, and you have beautiful hair. You, Strong Girl, have a beautiful heart! What makes you different, what makes you stand out, MAKES you beautiful.

Strong Girl, you have so many beautiful qualities.
Let's list 2 or 3 things you think are beautiful about you.

____

____

____

____

____

GOOD MORNING, STRONG GIRL.

WELCOME TO

Day six

- I am smart.
- I am smart.
- I am smart.

I take the time to study hard and make sure I do my homework daily.

Smart girls are Strong Girls. Smart is pretty, Smart is confident, Smart is you!

Keep in mind Strong Girl, you can't be a Smart Cookie
if you have a crumbly attitude !

List a few things you are doing to learn and grow.

GOOD MORNING, STRONG GIRL.

WELCOME TO

Day seven

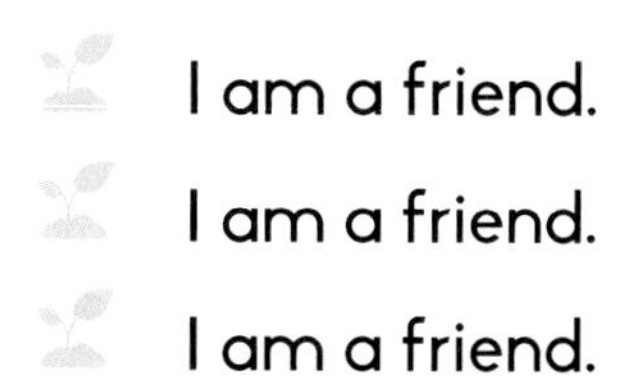

I am a friend.

I am a friend.

I am a friend.

I am a friend to others, no matter how they look or who they are, or what others say.

Strong Girls look for opportunities to be a friend to others.
Have lunch at school with someone new. Say hi to someone new.
Smile at someone new. I am a Friend!

I'm sure you can remember a time when you needed a friend.
What are some ways you have been a friend to someone?
How can you be a friend to someone who needs a friend?

Lessons LEARNED

About Honesty (by Desi)

A few days ago, this boy I know had somehow ruined his Pokémon cards. Since his cards were ruined, he asked me if I could help him get new ones. I said yes, because I wanted him to be my friend, and I wanted him to like me. So I asked my other friends if they could give me some Pokémon cards because I was starting my own collection. I ended up lying to a lot of my friends just to get free cards for this boy so he would be my friend. I wasn't thinking straight I guess.

I felt bad about it and ended up talking to my mom and dad about it. I decided that I would go purchase more Pokémon cards with the money I saved doing chores. With the new cards I bought, I made sure my friends got new ones in place of the ones I had gotten from them.

This whole Pokémon issue was a great lesson for me. From now on I am going to be honest. I don t need to impress people for them to be my friend. I didn't like the way it made me feel.

Love,
Desi

GOOD MORNING, STRONG GIRL.

WELCOME TO

Day eight

I am honest.

I am honest.

I am honest.

Being honest is the right thing to do. Sometimes we will make mistakes, however, it's important to be honest about our mistakes and take responsibility for them. Learn from your mistakes and move on. Strong Girls are honest.

If it's not right, don't do it.
If it's not true, don't say it!
Be true to yourself, keep honesty first place.

What are some ways you practice honesty? Have you ever felt bad when you weren't honest? How did it make you feel? Now learn from it.

GOOD MORNING, STRONG GIRL.

WELCOME TO

Day nine

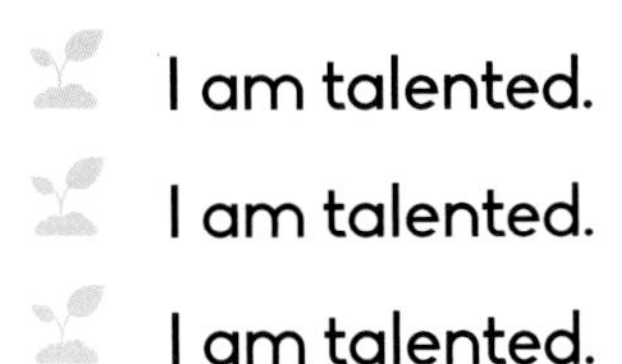

I am talented.

I am talented.

I am talented.

I can do anything I set my mind to.

If I practice, practice, and practice some more, and add in some hard work and imagination, the possibilities are limitless.

What **do** you love to do?
What specials talents do you have?
What **would** you love to do?
You are talented, Strong Girl!

GOOD MORNING, STRONG GIRL.

WELCOME TO

Day Ten

I am happy.

I am happy.

I am happy.

Did you know a smile is the best makeup any girl can wear?

Smile often. Smile right now. Smile because you can.
Turn that frown upside down Strong Girl.

Ah..Perfect, and oh how beautiful you are!

What makes you happy Strong Girl? What makes you smile?

Time to check in!

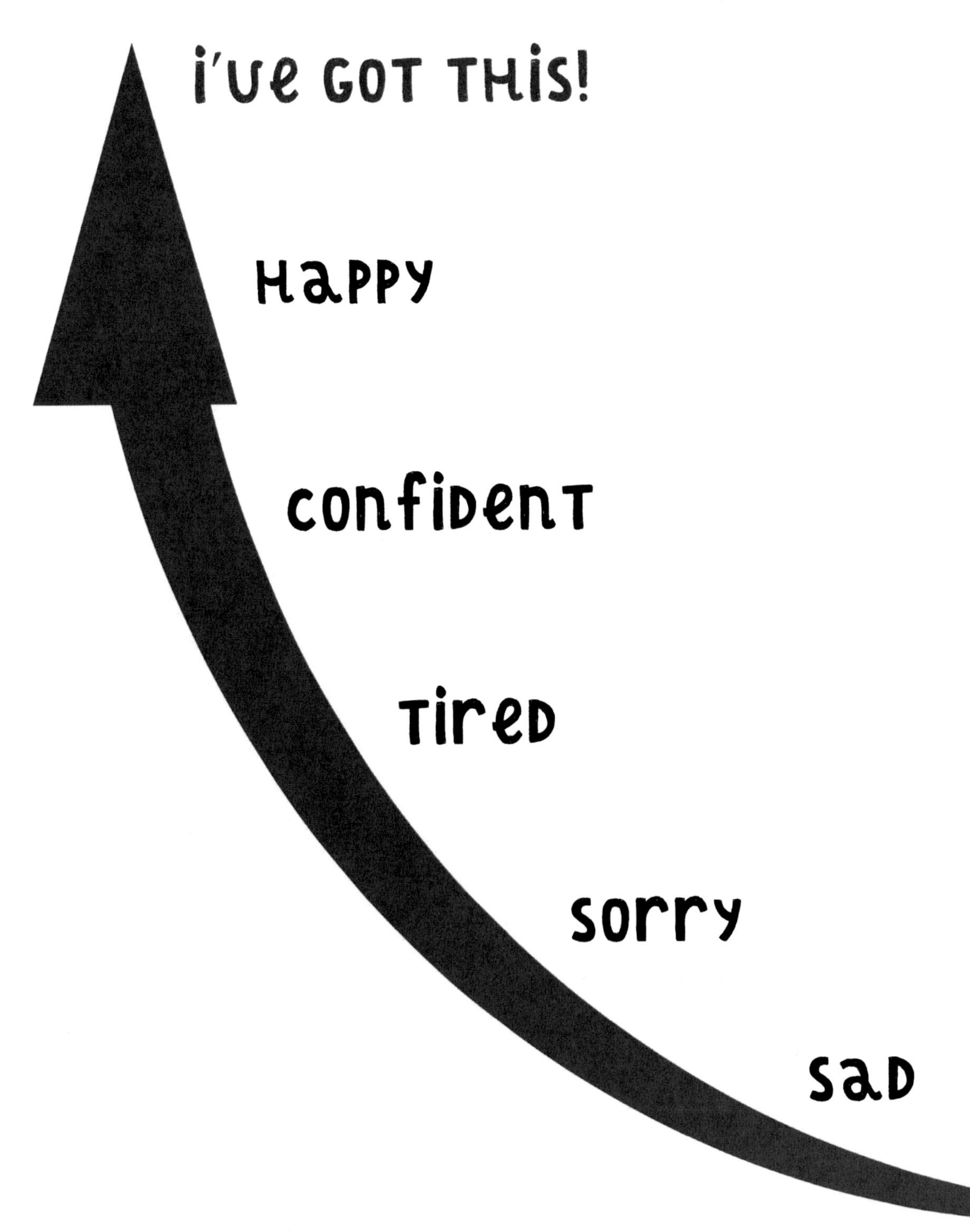

Circle how you are feeling right now. If you're in the bottom of the curve decide how you will climb to the top. You've got this, Strong Girl!

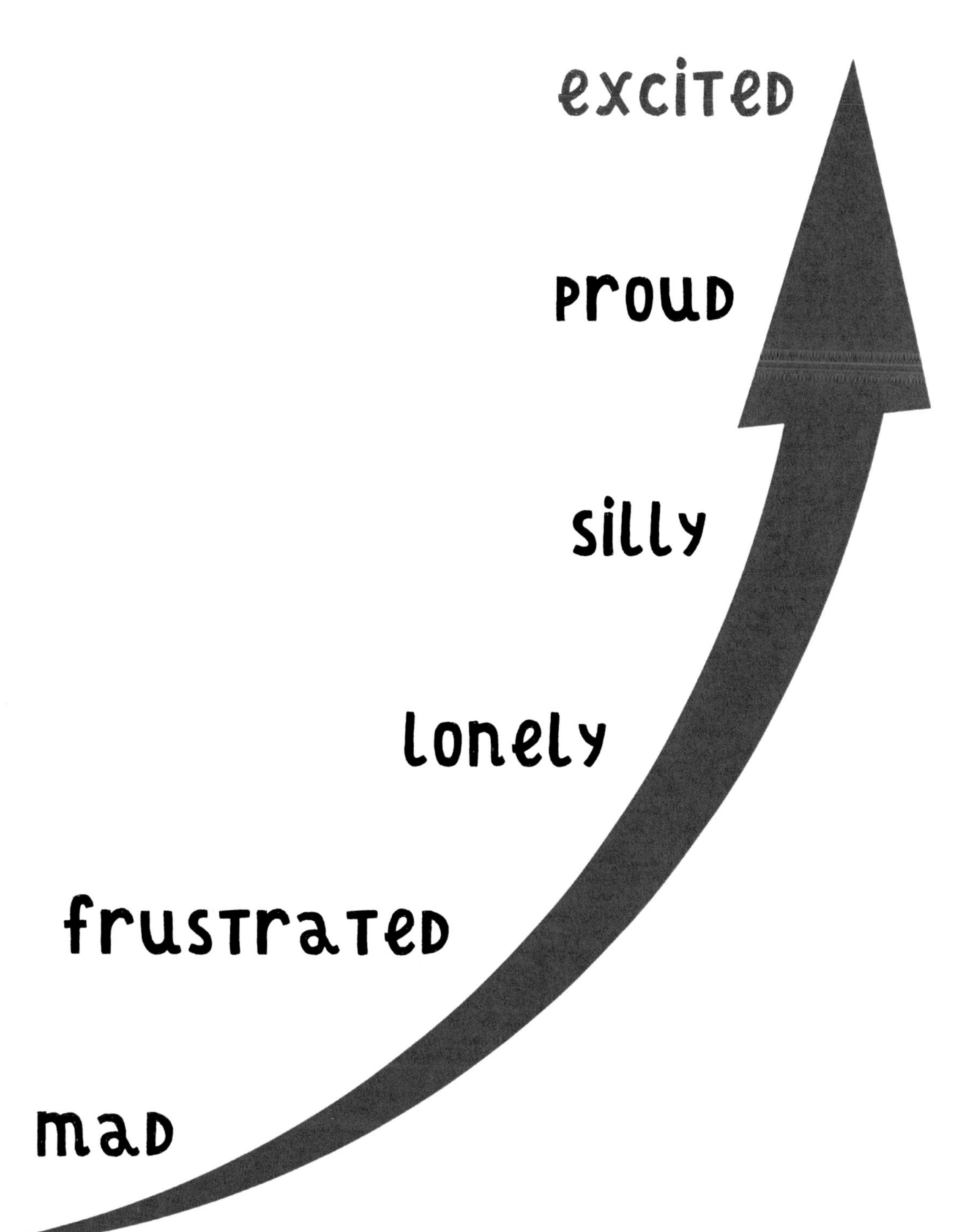

Lessons LEARNED

Being healthy.

If you are going to be your best, you must keep your energy up. If you are going to keep your energy up, you must be healthy. How do I do that, you ask? Get outside and play. Breathe in some fresh air and get some sunshine. Get plenty of rest, and if you are to get plenty of rest, you need to get to bed at a decent time. Strong Girl, that means 7-8 hours of sleep each night. You know when Mom or Dad tells you that you need your rest ... well guess what? They are right!

Exercise is important and it's as easy as getting in a walk, a run, swimming, jump roping, playing hopscotch, hula hooping, or getting outside to play. I bet you can come up with many other ways to get in some activity each day. When I was growing up I loved to skip. As a matter of fact, I still love to skip, it's fun!

List some things below that you can do to be healthy, and then get out and do them. Have fun!

GOOD MORNING, STRONG GIRL.

WELCOME TO

Day eleven

I am healthy.

I am healthy.

I am healthy.

I make healthy food choices to fuel my body. Healthy and strong is pretty.

Being healthy is important, however your worth is NOT determined by your body weight. Your worth is determined by who you are!

To be the best you can be, eat right, stay active, and get your sleep. Moving your body churns out good feelings and helps with positive seeds of strength. Your only limit is you! What did **you do today** to be healthy?

Lessons LEARNED

I am kind.

Sometimes kindness can be difficult. Sometimes we can be in a bad mood and not want to be kind. The real story here, Strong Girl, is that when we are unkind to our friends, family, or others, it's usually because we are not kind to ourselves.

To be kind to others, you must first start off by being kind to yourself. While this may be a different way to think about kindness, it is very important to start by being kind to yourself. Maybe you give yourself a big hug, or tell yourself a few times, "I am kind, I am kind, I am kind." Take a look in the mirror and tell yourself how amazing you are and how happy you are, even if you aren't happy in the moment. Just saying it will make it so, trust me! How about looking at some flowers or a tree or anything that just makes you smile. When you are kind to yourself, your kindness will spread to others around you, and that can start a movement of kindness everywhere.

What can you do today **to be kind to you?**

____

What can you do today **to be kind to someone else?**

____

GOOD MORNING, STRONG GIRL.

WELCOME TO

Day Twelve

I am kind.

I am kind.

I am kind.

GOOD MORNING, STRONG GIRL.

WELCOME TO

Day Thirteen

- I am thankful.
- I am thankful.
- I am thankful.

Thanksgiving is not the only time of year I should be thankful.
Strong Girls are thankful every day!

Every day I am thankful for the little things and the big things.
I am thankful for my mom, my dad, and my family. I am thankful for the sunshine, I am thankful for the rain, I am thankful for my warm bed, and I am thankful for my favorite books.

Now it's your turn. What are you thankful for?

GOOD MORNING, STRONG GIRL.

WELCOME TO

Day fourteen

I am courageous.

I am courageous.

I am courageous.

I will stand tall and be courageous even when there are days that are tough and bumps or hiccups come my way. I choose to be courageous.

Did you know Strong Girl, that this too shall pass and you **will** get past the tough bumps and hiccups of life and be much stronger because you were **courageous?**

Lessons LEARNED

Encourager Activity

You are an encourager, not just for yourself, but for your friends, your family, your brother, and your sister. What can you do today to encourage someone?

____

(Fill out the below section at the end of the day.)

Who did you encourage?

____

What did you do to encourage them?

____

How did it make them feel?

____

How did it make you feel?

____

GOOD MORNING, STRONG GIRL.

WELCOME TO

Day fifteen

I am an encourager.

I am an encourager.

I am an encourager.

I encourage my family and friends with positive thoughts and love. Everybody has seeds of strength, sometimes I just have to help them plant some.

What are some things that you currently do to help encourage others? What are some new ways you can help to encourage yourself? List these out.

GOOD MORNING, STRONG GIRL.

WELCOME TO

Day Sixteen

I am a learner.

I am a learner.

I am a learner.

I love to learn about new things. Learning helps me grow, learning helps me be the best me I can be.

Learning is fun! Learning is cool!

What did I learn new today? What else do I want to learn?

Lessons LEARNED

Joyful Activity

Being joyful is important, and it is also important to spread joyfulness to others. What can you do today, at school, at playtime, at home to spread joy? List one or two things you will do to bring joy to someone else.

____

(Answer the questions below at the end of the day.)

What you did to spread joy?

____

List how you felt spreading joy.

____

List how that person/s felt when you were spreading the joy.

____

List a way you can practice daily joyfulness.

____

Time to check in!

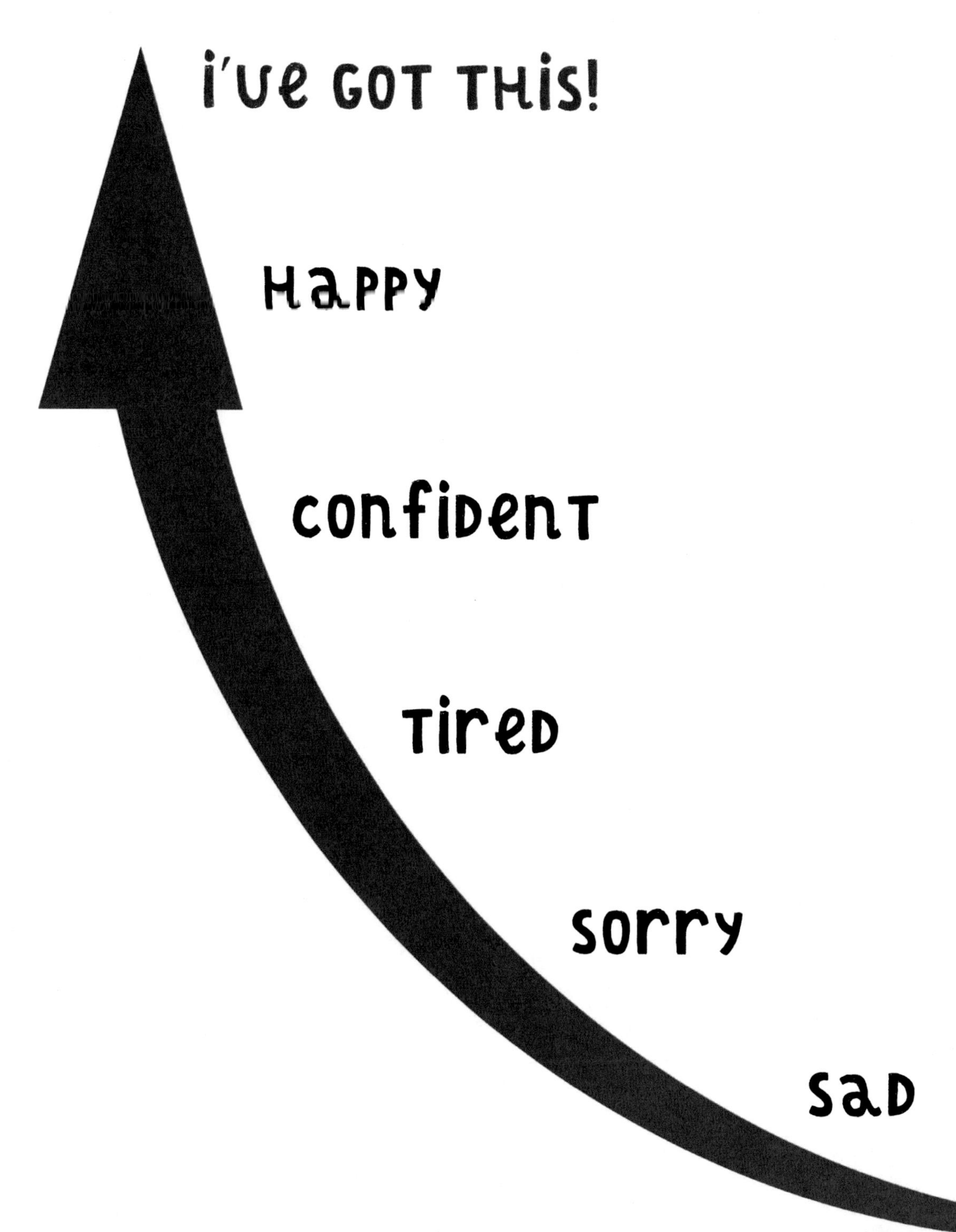

Circle how you are feeling right now. If you're in the bottom of the curve decide how you will climb to the top. You've got this, Strong Girl!

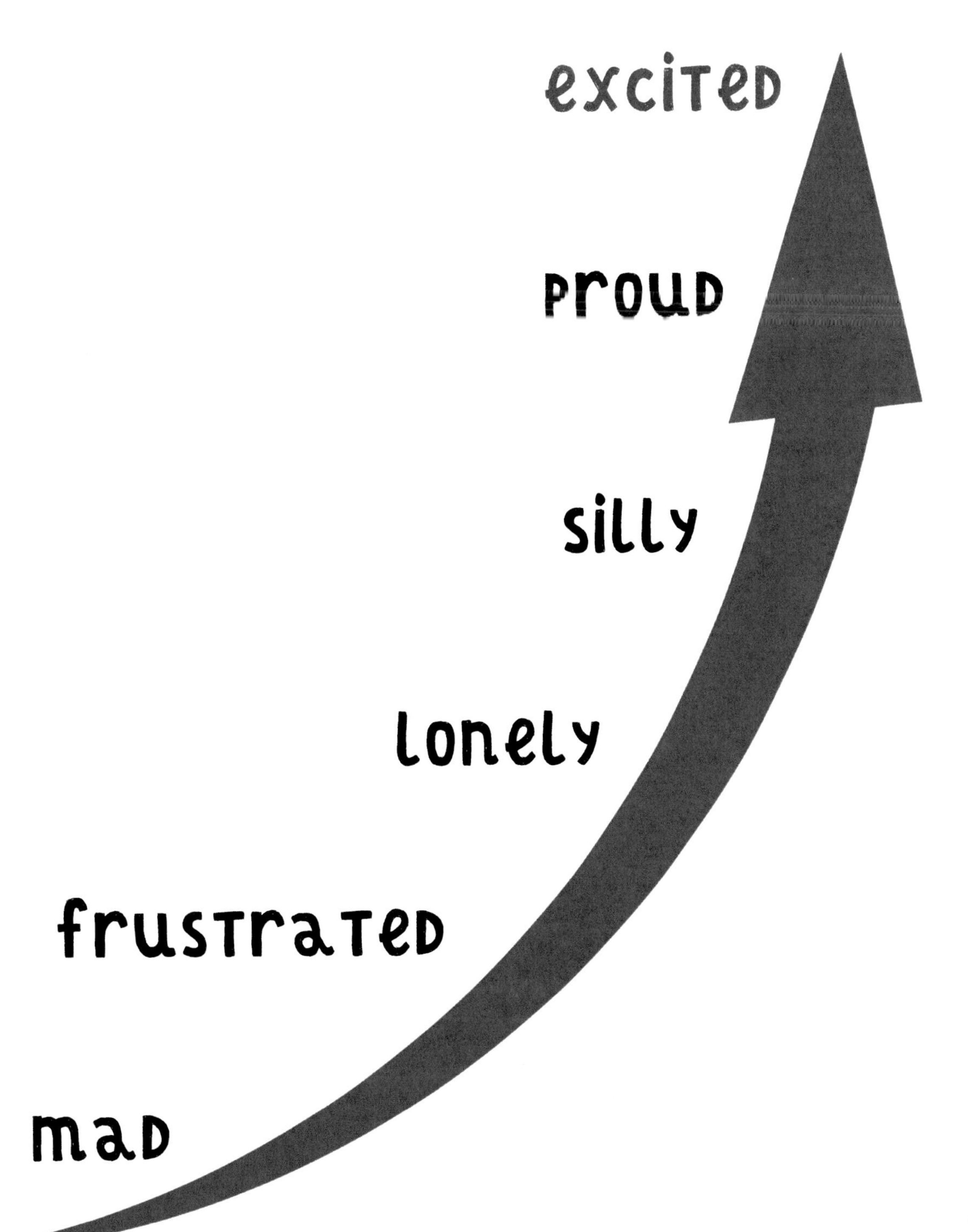

GOOD MORNING, STRONG GIRL.

WELCOME TO

Day Seventeen

- I am joyful.
- I am joyful.
- I am joyful.

I love to have fun, I love to laugh. I **will** laugh more often. Why not? Laughing and being full of joy is good for your mind, your heart and your body.

Being joyful is a choice. I choose to be joyful!

What are some fun/joyful things you like to do with your friends and family?

Lessons LEARNED

Being Excellent (by Rylee)

I am excellent in all I do.
I am excellent in all I do.
I am excellent in all I do.

Here's what I did to start being excellent:
Today I made my life plan board. I put all of my life goals on the life plan board, like people I want to meet, things I want to do, and places I want to go. I also put projects coming up and my schedule for soccer. This will help me to be organized and I won't miss anything or come unprepared. That's being excellent!

I really love my life board, it's the BEST! I just wanted to share with Grandma Terrie and your readers. You have inspired me to be my best. Thank you and love you!

Hugs and kisses,
Ry

GOOD MORNING, STRONG GIRL.

WELCOME TO

- I am excellent in all I do.
- I am excellent in all I do.
- I am excellent in all I do.

Growth doesn't happen by accident, it happens by being excellent in all you do! That means if you like to sing, dance, play soccer, tell stories, make friends, write poems, whatever it is, be EXCELLENT in what you are doing.

It doesn't mean you have to be the best at everything, it just means you try your hardest and give it your all. That's acting with **EXCELLENCE.**

What have you done today to bring your excellence?

GOOD MORNING, STRONG GIRL.

WELCOME TO

Day nineteen

I am in charge of how I feel.

I am in charge of how I feel.

I am in charge of how I feel.

There will be times, Strong Girl, when you may want to blame others for feeling sad or miserable. It's easy to want to blame others, but the truth is you can change how you feel about any situation or any negative feelings you are having.

Take charge for how you are feeling, you have a choice, so choose happiness.

Strong Girl, how are you feeling today?
If you are sad or bored, then what can **you do** to change that up?

GOOD MORNING, STRONG GIRL.

WELCOME TO

Day Twenty

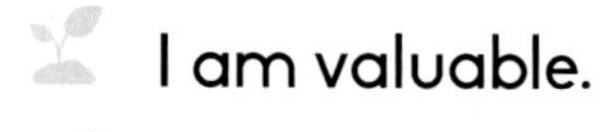

- I am valuable.
- I am valuable.
- I am valuable.

THE GREATEST HERO YOU CAN LOOK UP TO IS YOU!

There is a STRONG GIRL inside of every girl, and yes, that means you too!
Your value is not determined by what other people say, but rather by who YOU are!
The amazing, beautiful, smart you that you are!

Feeding yourself the daily seeds of positive strength helps you to build your value.

You are valuable, you are Strong Girl.
What are some things you tell yourself about your value?

____

____

____

____

GOOD MORNING, STRONG GIRL.
CONGRATULATIONS YOU ARE ON

Day Twenty One

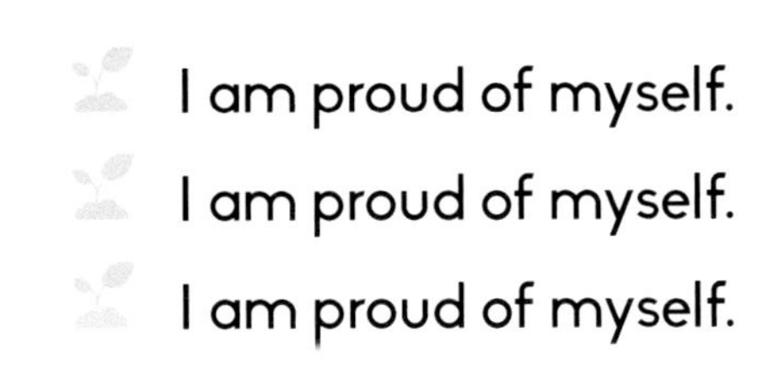

I am proud of myself.

I am proud of myself.

I am proud of myself.

I did it! I can do it. And if I fail I will just get up and try again.
Success is failure turned upside down.

Be proud of yourself, Strong Girl. You have taken a big step in daily discovery by planting your seeds of strength.

I am so proud of you for planting your daily seeds of strength, Strong Girl. Going forward, you've GOT THIS! What will you do next to keep your daily seeds of positivity watered and growing?

____

____

____

____

____

- - - - - - - - - -

favorite quotes for strong girls

"CHANGE your thoughts
& you CHANGE your
WORLD."

- norman vincent peale

"be the REASON
someone SMILES
TODAY."

- unknown

"When I was around eight,
I looked in the mirror and said,
You're either going to love
yourself or hate yourself.
AND I DECIDED
TO LOVE MYSELF.
That changed a lot of things."

- queen latifah

"we BECOME
what we think about."

- earl nightingale

"The more you PRAISE
& CELEBRATE your life,
the more there is in life to
CELEBRATE."

- Oprah Winfrey

"You are incredible, adorable, lovable, wonderful,
and PERFECTLY beautiful just the way you ARE."

-unknown

"be somebody who makes
EVERYBODY
FEEL LIKE
SOMEBODY."

-unknown

"GROW
where you are
planted."

-unknown

A positive **STRONG GIRL** attitude will determine your amazing positive direction.
CREATE your own sunshine Strong Girl and you **WILL DO GREAT THINGS!**

- always in Strong Girl spirit, Terrie Nathan

Where are you now?

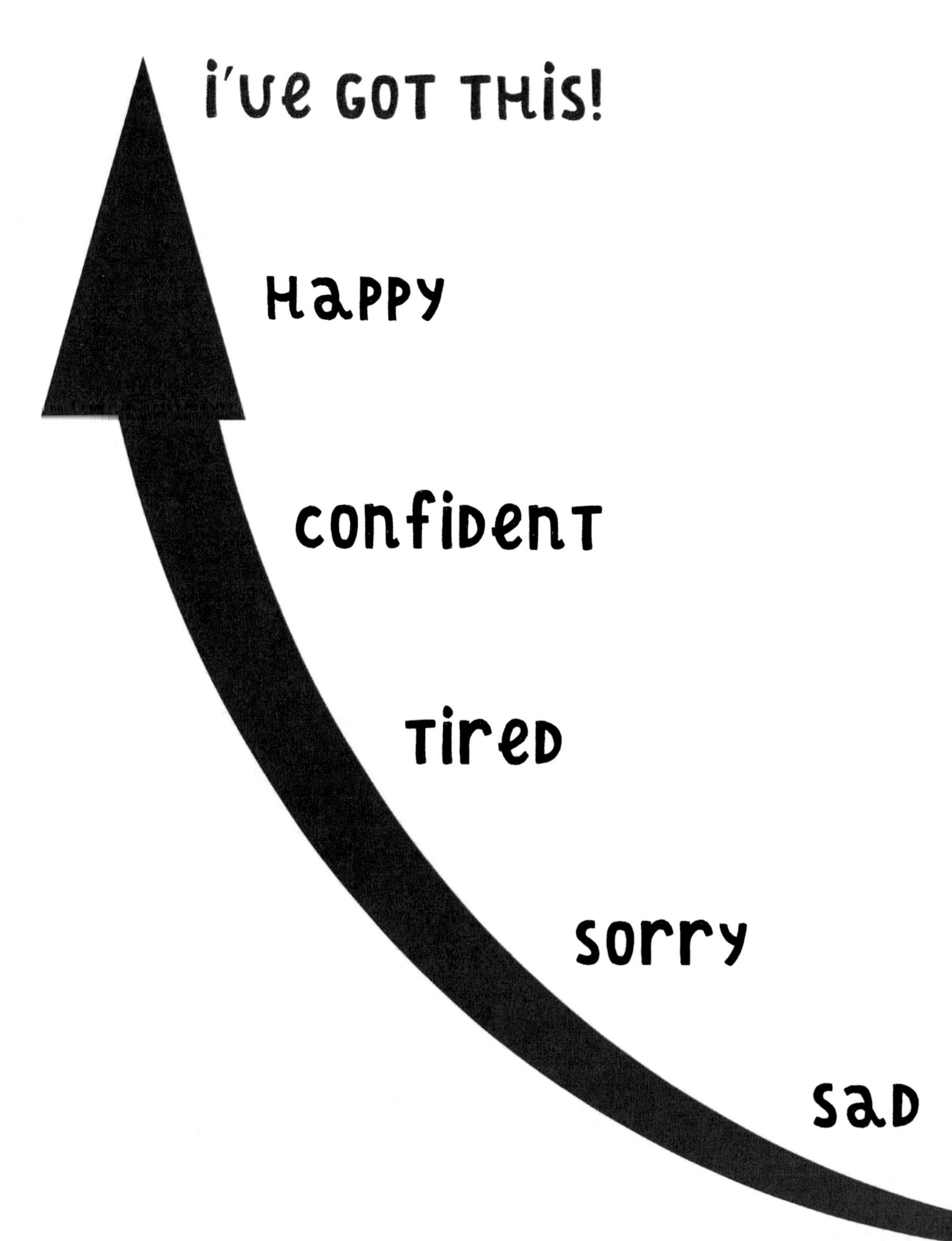

Circle how you are feeling right now. If you're in the bottom of the curve decide how you will climb to the top. You've got this, Strong Girl!

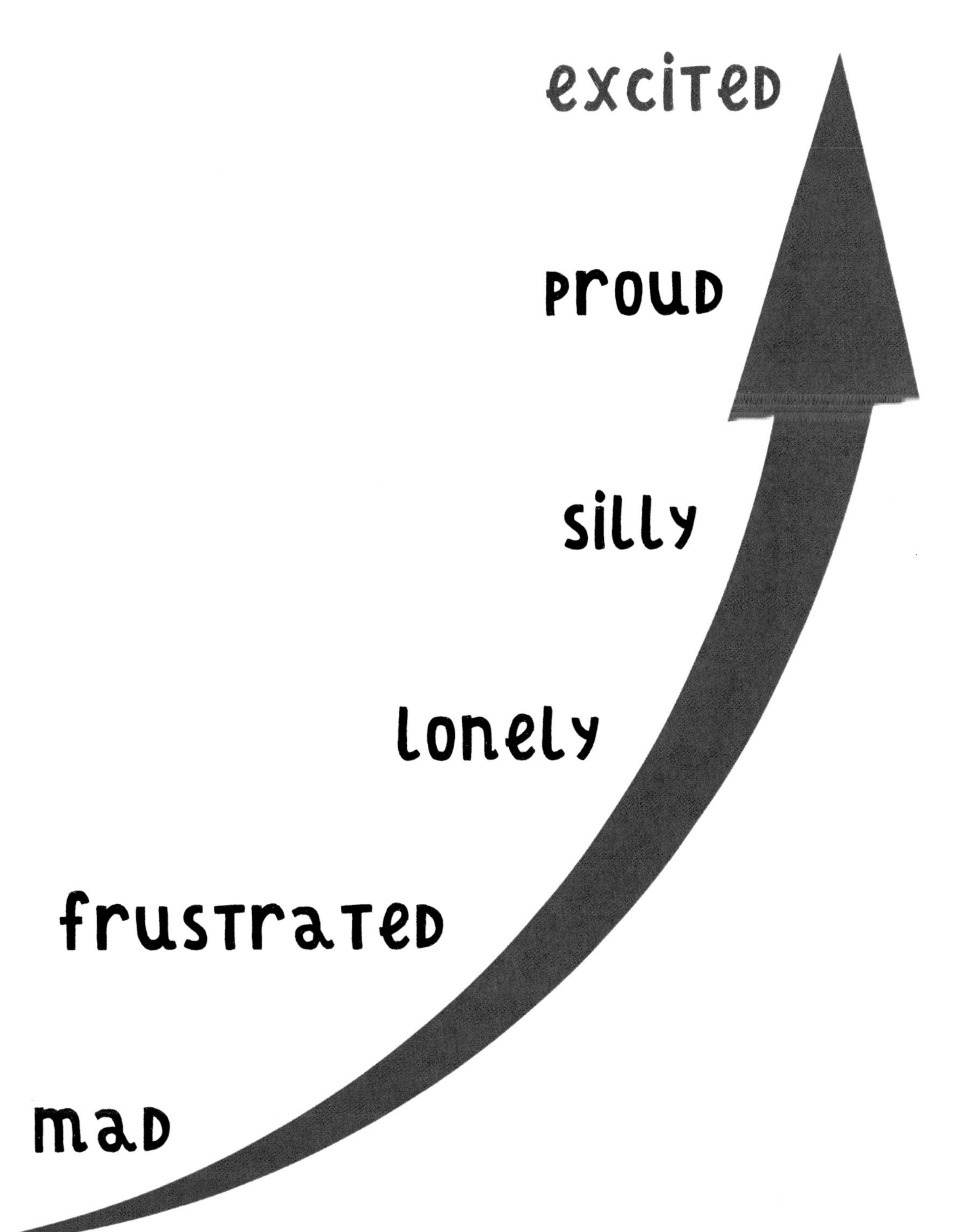

Lessons LEARNED

Write a Letter Activity

Write a letter to your older self and tell yourself how amazing, how wonderful, how excellent you will turn out. Say what it is you want to be in the future. After all, we become what we think about, so think big and be strong in your thinking. Here is my letter I wrote to myself when I was younger:

Dear Strong Girl,

I know sometimes life will be confusing to you. But I want you to stay strong and know that you are my hero. Whatever you might be going through is just part of growing up. Trust me, it will all work out, you must stay strong and love everything about you. You are beautiful, you are amazing, you are a bright light of confidence and love.

When life gets you down or things get to tough to stand, then kneel and pray because God is always listening. If for some reason you can t talk to Mom, Dad, your Brothers, or Friends, then know God is there for you. The more you talk things out with family, friends and God the more it all starts making sense. Life is full of bumps and bruises, so you must keep daily positive thoughts in front of you. You are Strong Girl and you will get past this stuff. Strong Girl you are awesome and even though you may not realize this right now, trust me, you will grow up and be a beautiful light of love, kindness, confidence, and strength! Life is good and you are never alone. Stay Strong my beautiful best friend! Go out and be AWESOME.

Loving you always,
Your Younger Self

now it's your turn!

WRITE YOUR LETTER BELOW.

about the author

Terrie Nathan
author & Strong Girl

TERRIE NATHAN is a #1 International Bestselling author. She draws her daily inspiration from every strong woman and girl out there. Her hope is to help spread the message of positive power across the world. In partnership with her support system, her family, she created this daily positive journal to help plant and grow individual seeds of strength in girls everywhere.

Terrie and her husband, Eric, live in Virginia Beach, VA and enjoy everything the beach life has to offer. Terrie's biggest fan, Eric, and two amazing adult children, Dean and Monica, are where she draws her strength, energy and desire to help Strong Girls everywhere. Terrie's son, Dean, and his wife, Mary, are the terrific parents of Rylee and Desi (Terrie's beautiful granddaughters). The family all share a passion for people and understand the importance of daily positive reinforcement in our own lives and the lives of others.

Please share your positive stories regarding your seeds of strength!

VISIT StrongGirlSpirit.com | EMAIL terrie@stronggirlspirit.com

@stronggirlspirit

@strong_girl_spirit

@stronggirl52

@stronggirl

Made in the USA
Columbia, SC
16 May 2019